CHARLIE BROWN
Not Your Average Blockhead

by

SCHULZ

HarperCollins*Publishers*

Charlie Brown: Not Your Average Blockhead

HarperCollins Publishers
Produced by Jennifer Barry Design, Sausalito, CA
Creative consultation by 360°, NYC.
First published in 1997 by HarperCollins*Publishers* Inc.
http://www.harpercollins.com

Creative and Editorial Director: Jennifer Barry
Editor: Kristen Schilo
Design Assistant: Kristen Wurz

ISBN 0-06-757518-8

Printed in Hong Kong

1 3 5 7 9 10 8 6 4 2

Many thanks to the following dedicated and invaluable contributors to this book:

Liz Conyngham, Susannah Craig, John Douglas, Evelyn Ellison, Theresa Fitzgerald, Ken Fund, Alex George, Chris Goff, Ellen Hogan, Heide Inglese, Amy Lago, Steven Masur, Helen Moore, Lorrie Myers, Andrea Podley, Edna Poehner, Erin Samuels, Charles M. Schulz, Jeannie Schulz, John Silbersack, Patricia Teberg, Meg Troy and the staffs at 360°, NYC, Creative Associates, HarperCollins Publishers Inc., Jennifer Barry Design and United Media.

Contents

Foreword

Charlie Brown…my friend and my own personal hero. He is sensitive, caring, humble and tenacious. What I love so much about him is, this round-headed kid never gives up! Whether he is dealing with his precocious pooch, pining for a certain little red-haired girl, trying to kick a football held by Lucy or losing another baseball game, Charlie Brown has little control over his universe.

One of the reasons I love Charlie Brown so much is he's a supremely decent person. Granted, he's no more than pen and ink on newsprint, yet consider this amazing fact: he and his comic strip are still tremendously popular after almost 50 years. So much for being an average blockhead! Charlie Brown isn't average at all.

Charlie Brown is our ray of sunshine. He is a true survivor. He has the hope and courage of people who know the glass is half-full. Isn't that what life is all about? Getting up in the morning and making the most of what you have? Bless you, Charlie Brown. You'll always be my favorite blockhead *and* inspiration.

Andrea Podley
Founder and Editor of the
Peanuts Collectors Club, Inc.

Introduction

My original submission to United Feature Syndicate was a series of what we call "gag characters," in other words, a panel which would have different characters each day. When I went to New York to discuss the possible sale and arrangement of the feature, they discovered that I could also draw a regular comic strip and they indicated that this would be something they would

prefer. They told me, of course, that if we started a new comic strip I would have to create some definite characters. This was actually good news to me for I much preferred doing a strip.

I had no trouble thinking of two or three characters, one of them being a little dog. The lead character would be a round-headed kid with a rather plain face and I decided he should be called Charlie Brown. I was afraid, however,

that the Syndicate editor wouldn't understand that the other characters would always be calling him by his full name and I was surprised when he agreed that it would work.

At this time, I was working at the correspondence school, Art Instruction, Inc. and one of my closest friends, who also worked there, was named Charlie

Brown. I had been there for about a year before he was hired and when he arrived everyone called him Charlie. He was a very bright young man with a lot of enthusiasm for life.

As we got to know each other better, to the point where we could joke about many things, I began to tease him about his love for parties and I used to say, "Here comes good ol' Charlie Brown, now we can have a good time."

Soon everyone began to refer to him as Charlie Brown.

So when I created this new character I thought it was only considerate to ask for permission to use his name. He seemed to think it was all right and I remember the day he crossed the room from his desk to mine, looked down at the character I was drawing and said, "What a disappointment, I thought I was going to look more like Steve Canyon."

As the years went by, many humorous things happened to my friend Charlie because of the comic-strip name and I began to feel a bit guilty for fear I was causing him trouble. But, as one of our other friends remarked, "Don't worry about it, he is also having a lot of fun." In fact, one time he was invited to go to New York and appear on a television show called *To Tell The Truth* where a panel had to guess who the real Charlie Brown was and he fooled them all.

Many things have happened to me during these past years because of *Peanuts*, but one of the most gratifying memories has always been my friendship with "good ol' Charlie Brown."

Charles M. Schulz
Summer 1997

Classic

Charlie Brown

He's been known as a blockhead, said to be wishy-washy, and often says "Good Grief!," but to most fans, he is known as "Good ol' Charlie Brown." As the big brother to Sally and a friend to the others in the gang, Charlie Brown is the type of person lots of people like to give advice to—especially Lucy. Whether or not he follows it, he at least listens and thinks about it.

He believes the reason for his strange state is that he has missed all the rehearsals in life and wonders if there are side effects of being happy. He often sits under a big tree with Snoopy which does Chuck some good—it is there that he decides that "having a dog for a friend can make an ordinary life a beautiful life." A wonderful sentiment for someone who is supposedly a blockhead!

Charlie Brown has a spirit which constantly challenges the adversity set before him. He is the losing pitcher and part-time popcorn vendor on the baseball field, but also the manager and fearless leader of the team. He is referred to by Snoopy as "the round-headed kid," but he is also Snoopy's master and loyal best friend. No matter how many strikes there are against him, Charlie Brown seems to triumph.

"I never seem to know

what's going on..."

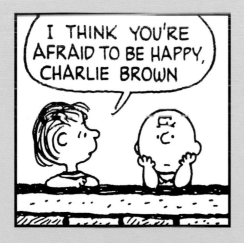

"I'd like to be the sort of

likes to have around."

person that everyone

"*I worry about all*

the wrong things . . . "

"...I don't know any

thing about love..."

29

"...*I've always wanted*

to have a good time..."

"*...I never know what*

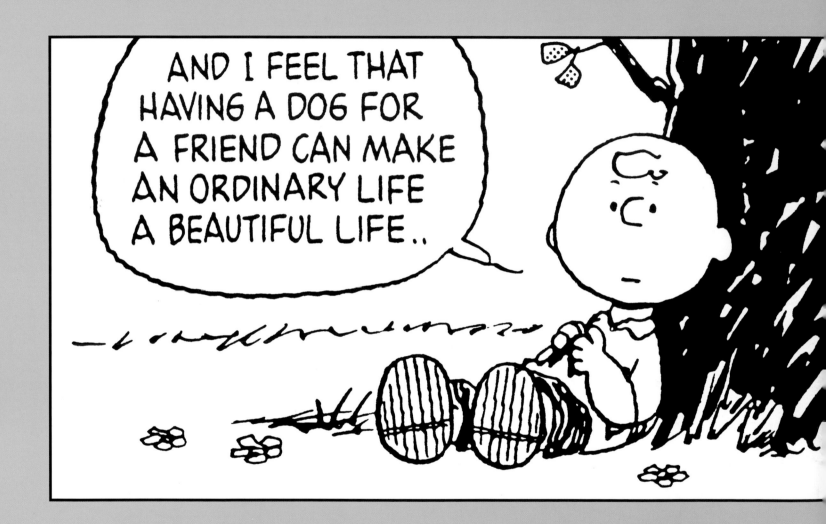

my dog is thinking."

YUK YUK YUK YUK YUK YUK

YUK YUK YUK YUK YUK YUK

Lovable

Charlie Brown

A hopeless romantic at heart, Charlie Brown ponders love and is a firm believer that "love makes you do strange things." When he takes a walk, his body is often startled by something his mind has just conjured up—he is reminded of a lost love or a relationship that just cannot get off the ground.

Charlie Brown could be called the Knight of Unrequited Love, as he pines for the Little Red-Haired Girl day after day. As he tries to get her to notice him, he ends up embarrassing himself by getting sent to the eye doctor for winking at cute girls or getting his mittens frozen to a tree.

Although Peppermint Patty and Marcie harbor not-so-secret crushes on their friend, Charlie Brown has trouble responding to the attention these gals give him. He claims to know less about love the older he gets and claims that Snoopy knows more about it than he does.

Whether he is waiting under his mailbox or inside it—valentines never seem to come to his address. Instead of thinking that he is the only person in the world who never gets love letters, he deems himself as the leader of the millions just like him—Good ol' Charlie Brown!

"Love makes you

do strange things"

IF I WINK AT THAT LITTLE RED HAIRED GIRL, MAYBE SHE'LL NOTICE ME

WHERE'RE YOU GOING, CHARLIE BROWN?

THE TEACHER WANTS ME TO SEE THE NURSE ABOUT MY EYE

SHE SAW ME WINKING AT THE LITTLE RED HAIRED GIRL.. SHE THINKS SOMETHING'S WRONG WITH MY EYE...

WHAT AM I GOING TO TELL THE NURSE?

I CAN'T BELIEVE THIS IS HAPPENING..

I WINK AT THAT LITTLE RED HAIRED GIRL..THE TEACHER SENDS ME TO THE NURSE..THE NURSE SENDS ME TO THE EYE DOCTOR...

I'M LUCKY I DIDN'T TRY TO GIVE HER A HUG...

THEY'D HAVE SENT ME TO AN ORTHOPEDIST TO FIX MY ARMS!

DID YOU GO TO THE EYE DOCTOR YESTERDAY, CHARLIE BROWN?

YES, HE SAID THERE'S NOTHING WRONG WITH MY EYES..THEY'RE FINE..

DID HE TELL YOU TO STOP WINKING AT GIRLS?

HE SAID THAT'S THE FIRST THING THEY TEACH YOU IN MEDICAL SCHOOL

"...I thought love was sup

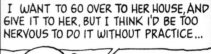

Philosophical

Charlie Brown

Late-night worries and pondering the meaning of life are common for us all—especially Charlie Brown. While in bed, with his faithful beagle at his feet, he worries about school, getting valentines, his losing baseball team, and what might happen to him tomorrow. All of his worrying usually ends up being for naught, but at least it keeps him busy!

Charlie Brown often sits by the wall with his pal Linus and ponders what life has in store for them. Their discussions lead to self-awareness, and their questions and despair frequently turn into glimpses of wisdom.

Our hero is as up as he is down, something that Charlie Brown himself refers to as "being suspended from the bungee cord of life." As he sits and watches the world go by, Charlie Brown expresses the same fear of the unknown that we all have contemplated at one time or another. Forever the optimist, Charlie Brown has said, "Tomorrow will be a new day and we never know what excitement lies ahead."

Sometimes I lie

and ask myself, "Is

awake at night

this all there is?"

"*...but remember, tomor*

row is another day."

SOMETIMES I LIE AWAKE AT NIGHT, AND I THINK ABOUT THE GOOD LIFE THAT I HAVE .. I REALLY HAVE NO COMPLAINTS..

THEN A VOICE COMES TO ME FROM OUT OF THE DARK, "WE APPRECIATE YOUR ATTITUDE!"

Sporting

Charlie Brown

Charlie Brown finds success on the sports field as often as he does in other aspects of his life, almost never. Year after year, Charlie Brown runs to kick the football, and year after year, Lucy pulls it away from him. Aaugh! Will he ever learn?

Baseball eludes him too. He tries to use the ol' schmuckle ball to strike out the opposing team, but how can this pitcher ever win with a pitch taught to him by Lucy? Practically every game he spends disheveled on the mound, with his clothes up in the air. How can he gain respect from his team?

Charlie Brown gains respect because he endures. Even when he gets his kite tangled up by the kite-eating tree for the umpteenth time, he keeps going. He exemplifies the "good sport" because whether it is sunny, raining or snowing, our hero will be on the field, even without his team! His optimism is endless and what makes us all love him so.

"*Life is a lot like a*

baseball game…"

Sporting Charlie Brown

OVER HERE! I'M OVER HERE!

I CAN'T BELIEVE IT...

NOT AGAIN!

DOES SHE REALLY THINK I'M SUCH A FOOL? NOT AGAIN!

AM I DUMB ENOUGH TO THINK SHE'S GOING TO LET ME KICK THAT FOOTBALL? I CAN'T BELIEVE IT! NOT AGAIN!

"*Every time you think*

things can't get any

worse..."

WHAT COULD BE WORSE THAN BEING TANGLED IN A KITE STRING AND HANGING UPSIDE DOWN FROM A TREE?